HAL•LEONARD
INSTRUMENTAL
PLAY-ALONG

AUDIO ACCESS INCLUDED

PLAYBACK+
Speed • Pitch • Balance • Loop

HORN

CHRISTMAS CLASSICS

Audio arrangements by Peter Deneff

To access audio visit:
www.halleonard.com/mylibrary

Enter Code
1137-7243-8593-0566

ISBN 978-1-4950-7059-4

HAL•LEONARD®
CORPORATION
7777 W. BLUEMOUND RD. P.O. BOX 13819 MILWAUKEE, WI 53213

In Australia Contact:
Hal Leonard Australia Pty. Ltd.
4 Lentara Court
Cheltenham, Victoria, 3192 Australia
Email: ausadmin@halleonard.com.au

Visit Hal Leonard Online at
www.halleonard.com

ANGELS WE HAVE HEARD ON HIGH

HORN

Traditional French Carol

BRING A TORCH, JEANNETTE, ISABELLA

HORN

17th Century French Provençal Carol

COVENTRY CAROL

HORN

Traditional English Melody

FUM, FUM, FUM

HORN

Traditional Catalonian Carol

GO, TELL IT ON THE MOUNTAIN

HORN

African-American Spiritual

GOD REST YE MERRY, GENTLEMEN

HORN

Traditional English Carol

HERE WE COME A-CAROLING

HORN

Traditional

THE HOLLY AND THE IVY

HORN

18th Century English Carol

I SAW THREE SHIPS

HORN

Traditional English Carol

JINGLE BELLS

HORN

Words and Music by
J. PIERPONT

O COME, ALL YE FAITHFUL

HORN

Music by JOHN FRANCIS WADE

O HOLY NIGHT

HORN

French Words by PLACIDE CAPPEAU
English Words by JOHN S. DWIGHT
Music by ADOLPHE ADAM

SILENT NIGHT

HORN

Words by JOSEPH MOHR
Music by FRANZ X. GRUBER

STILL, STILL, STILL

HORN

Salzburg Melody, c.1819

WHAT CHILD IS THIS?

HORN

16th Century English Melody